Brainteaser
Puzzles **2**

Pocket**Puzzles**

Capella

This edition published in 2007 by Arcturus Publishing Limited
26/27 Bickels Yard, 151–153 Bermondsey Street,
London SE1 3HA

In Canada published for Indigo Books
468 King St W,
Suite 500,
Toronto,
Ontario M5V 1L8

Copyright © 2007 Arcturus Publishing Limited

ISBN: 1-84193-678-2
ISBN: 978-1-84193-678-9

Printed in China

Introduction

This compilation is packed full of visual, word and number puzzles designed to entertain and test you at the same time. The puzzles should help develop your ability to think laterally, although do remember that they are not IQ tests and that you may find some puzzles easier than others. The puzzles vary in difficulty and are not arranged in any particular order, but you will find a good mix throughout the book.

The solutions to the puzzles are at the back of the book, but we recommend that you only check them if you really need to: it really is much more fun to try to work out the answers for yourself!

Give values for X and Y.

Which is the odd one out?

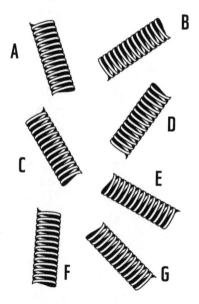

Which is the odd one out?

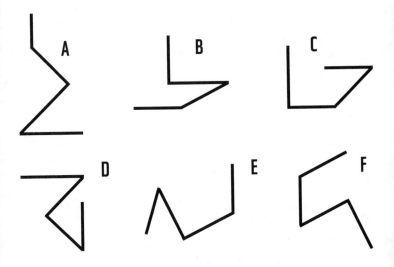

What number goes into the empty brackets?

98 (79) 126
105 (79) 135
48 (35) 80
34 ( ) 85

What numbers should replace the letters A, B and C?

```
3 A 6
C 4 B
B 2 B A
```

What number should replace the letter X?

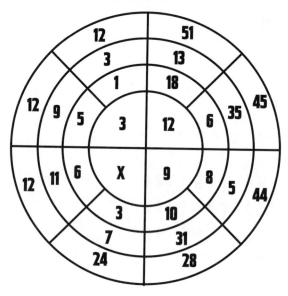

7

Which number in the bottom line comes next in the top line?

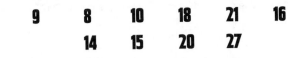

9   8   10   18   21   16   –

14   15   20   27

8

What comes next in this series?

1 7 8 15 23 38 61 –

9

What number should replace the letter X?

25 22 15 X 10 19 24

Barbara visited her High School friend, Natasha after their 25th school reunion. "What a nice pair of children you have, are they twins?", Barbara asked.

"No my sister is older than I," said Natasha's son Philip. "The square of my age plus the cube of her age is 7148."

"The square of my age plus the cube of his age is 5274," said Matilda.

How old were they?

Group these six figures into three pairs.

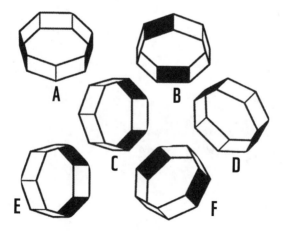

Group these symbols into five sets of three.

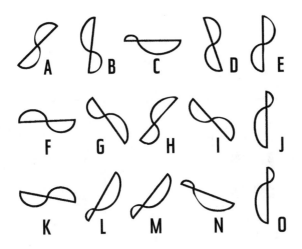

A train moving at 49 mph meets and is passed by a train moving at 63 mph.
A passenger in the first train noted that the second train took 4.5 seconds to pass him.

How long is the second train?

Multiply the numbers that are midway between the lowest and highest numbers in A and B and subtract the midway number in C.

5	4	97
6	95	99
3	98	96

A

77	8	75
9	76	10
79	7	74

B

10	9	76
75	77	12
73	11	74

C

What goes into the empty square?

0	7	2	4	12	6	3
7	9	6		18	9

The 1st man has 16 sapphires
The 2nd man has 10 emeralds
The 3rd man has 8 diamonds

Each man gives the other two, two of his gems and then all 3 have the same value of wealth.

What are the individual values of the three types of jewels?

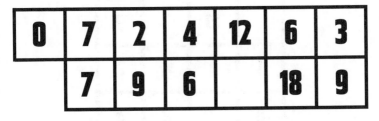

	10	7	3
1	4	15	11
8		2	6
16		5	9

Apart from the numbers 12,13 and 14, the numbers 1-16 have been inserted into the grid almost, but not quite, at random.

Following just two simple rules, where would you place the numbers 12,13 and 14 in the grid?

The crocodile had a tail that was three times as long as its head and its body was half as long as its tail.

Its body and tail measured 171 inches.

How long was its head?

A man had to pack apples in packets, but as each packet has to have exactly the same number of apples, he was having difficulty.

If he packed 10 apples in a packet, one packet had only 9

"	9	"	"		8
"	8	"	"		7
"	7	"	"		6

and so on, down to

"	2	"	"		1

How many apples did he have?

The porter had mixed up the room keys. There are 20 rooms. What is the maximum number of trials required to sort out the keys?

Which is the odd one out?

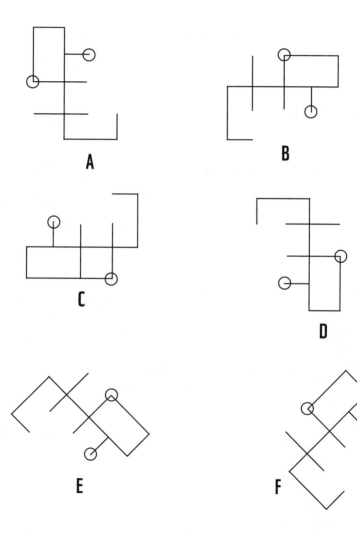

A

B

C

D

E

F

Clue: Spindrift skimmers! (4-7)

Find the (4-7) letter words. Find the 1st letter. Draw a straight line
to the 2nd letter, then to the 3rd letter and so on. The enclosed
areas have been filled in.

Which hexagon fits the space?

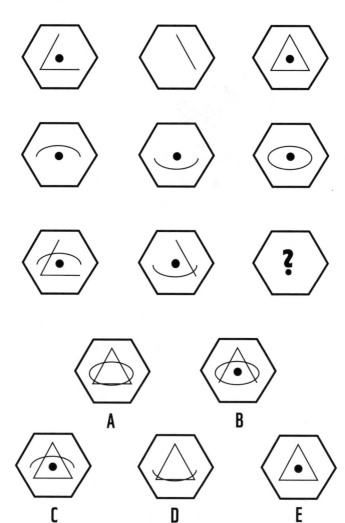

If the two figures at the top are correct, which of those below are wrong?

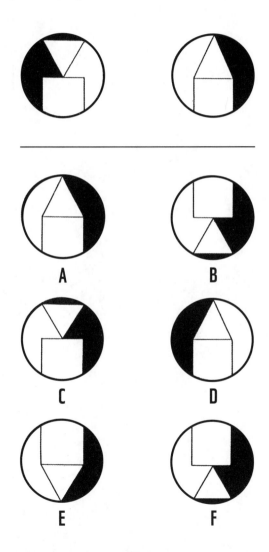

Which tumbler is wrong?

A   B   C   D

E   F   G   H

I   J   K   L

Which one is wrong?

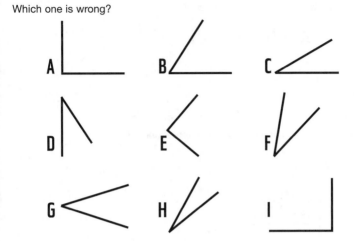

What is the last term in this series?

B 2 T 20 Q 17 G 7 C –

What number should replace the letter X ?

4   9   X   25

What numbers should replace the letters X and Y?

5	20
8	J
W	25
16	T
A	4
5	K
C	7
X	L
A	Y
4	N

Replace the letters with numbers.

TWELVE
TWELVE
TWELVE
TWELVE
TWELVE
+ THIRTY
———————
NINETY

A rotates clockwise all the time, one position at a time. If it stops on an odd number, ball B moves one place anti-clockwise; if A stops on an even number, B moves three places clockwise. If ball B stops on an even number, ball C moves three places clockwise; if B stops on an odd number, C moves five places anti-clockwise.

At the end of six moves what place will be spelled out by ball C?

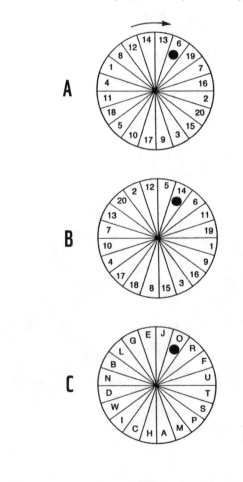

What set of numbers comes next?

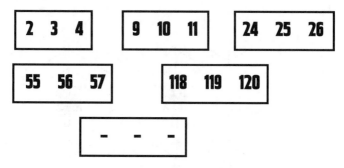

| 2 3 4 | 9 10 11 | 24 25 26 |

| 55 56 57 | 118 119 120 |

| – – – |

Can you discover six male forenames in the outer ring and six female names in the inner ring?

Which is the odd one out?

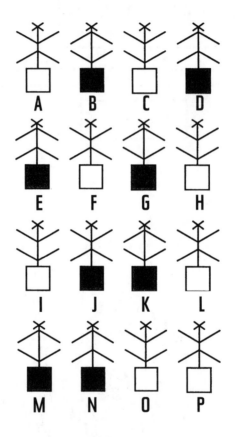

Which of the figures at the bottom should follow number 3 at the top?

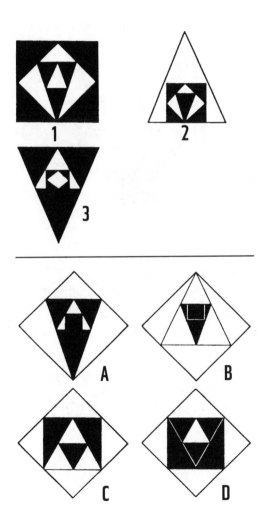

What number should replace the letter X?

4 9 13 2 2 3 5 5 7 9 X

Here is part of a jigsaw puzzle on which a triangle is marked. Which is the missing piece?

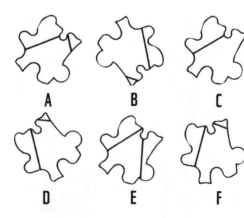

Here is a roulette wheel. When the ball stops at zero all the stakes go to the casino. The ball travels anti-clockwise. At the first spin it stops at the next number. Then it misses one and stops at the next. After that each spin brings the ball one extra number along (missing two, then three, and so on). At what spin will the stakes go to the casino?

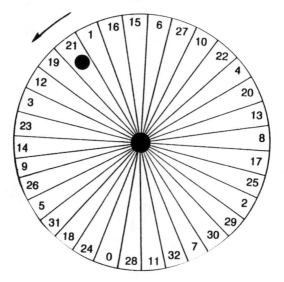

Which of the figures at the bottom belongs to E?

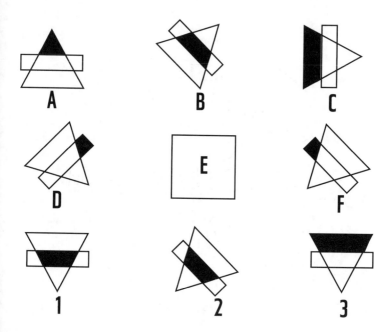

Six of these keys will open the door. Which one won't?

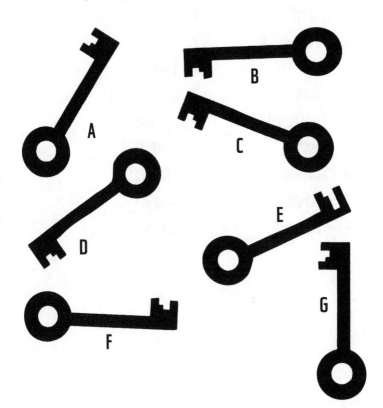

Pair these words to make nine titles of books by Charles Dickens:

A	**LITTLE**	**1**	**RUDGE**
B	**PICKWICK**	**2**	**COPPERFIELD**
C	**EDWIN**	**3**	**TIMES**
D	**BARNABY**	**4**	**CHUZZLEWIT**
E	**NICHOLAS**	**5**	**PAPERS**
F	**HARD**	**6**	**HOUSE**
G	**BLEAK**	**7**	**DROOD**
H	**DAVID**	**8**	**DORRIT**
I	**MARTIN**	**9**	**NICKLEBY**

Which screw is different?

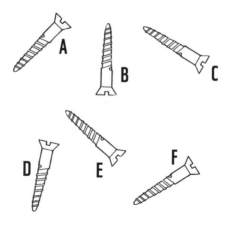

Which of the figures below should occupy the vacant space?

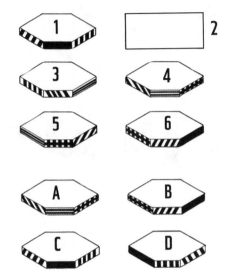

What number goes into the empty brackets?

916 (160) 916

971 (177) 879

245 ( ) 511

Arrange these into four pairs.

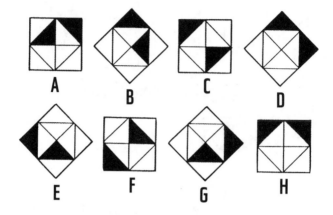

What goes into the empty space?

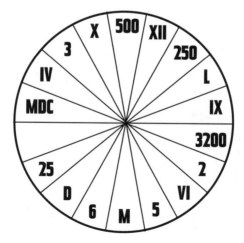

Which cube at the bottom should follow the two at the top?

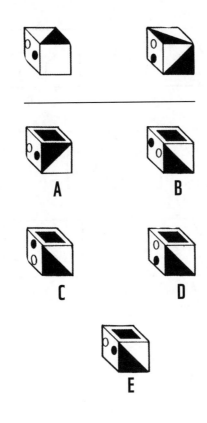

A

B

C

D

E

Complete this series, giving a value for X.

11 13 17 25 32 37 47 58 X 79

If A were superimposed on top of B which of the outlines below would result?

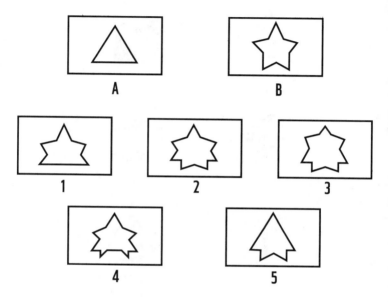

What number should replace the question mark?

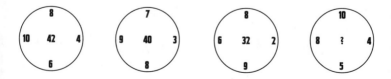

Clue: You need this to run before the wind. (9)

Find the (9) letter word. Find the 1st letter. Draw a straight line to the 2nd letter, then to the 3rd letter and so on. The enclosed areas have been filled in.

Complete this sequence:

2 3 4 9 16 81 256

How many revolutions of cog 1 will take place in order to bring the black teeth into mesh with the black tooth of cog 2:

A If 1 rotates clockwise

B If 2 rotates clockwise?

Simplify (x-y)2

Choose from

A. $- x^2 - 2xy + y^2$
B. $x^2 - 2xy + y^2$
C. $x^2 - 2xy - y^2$
D. $x^2 + 2xy - y^2$
E. $-x^2 + 2xy + y^2$

Which of these is the odd one out?

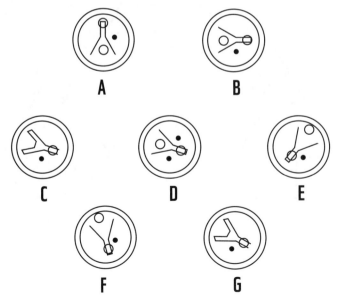

A

B

C

D

E

F

G

Which figure is the odd one out?

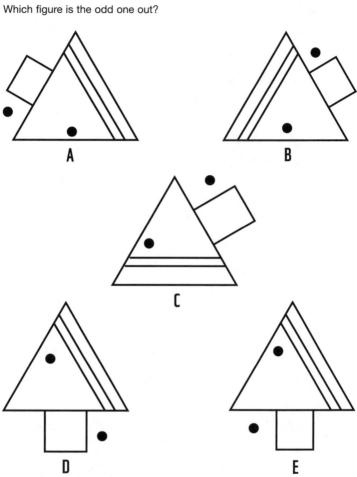

A

B

C

D

E

These are the recognized names given to groups of creatures, but they have been mixed up. You have to re-arrange them correctly.

Colony of Birds

Horde of Spiders

Den of Wild Pigs

Clutter of Crows

Nest of Snakes

Park of Elks

Doylt of Ferrets

Gang of Machine Guns

Business of Swine

Volery of Artillery

Hover of Gnats

Drift of Frogs

You don't have to be a motorist to solve this. Minimum stopping distances are as follows:

at 20mph ... 40 feet

at 30mph ... 75 feet

at 40mph ... 120 feet

at 50mph ... 175 feet

at 60mph ... 240 feet

at 70mph ... 315 feet

When following another vehicle a gap of one yard (three feet) for every mile per hour MAY be sufficient.

At what speed would this gap exactly correspond with the minimum stopping distance?

What is the total of the spots on the rear sides of these dice?

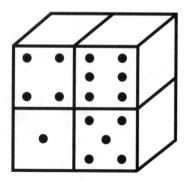

Which of the four squares at the bottom should follow square 4?

8	2	3	6
2	6	7	4
7	6	4	2
2	5	5	7

1

4	9	1	4
3	6	6	3
7	1	8	2
4	2	3	9

2

3	8	1	5
5	3	5	4
4	2	9	2
5	4	2	6

3

3	9	3	1
4	3	4	5
6	1	5	4
3	3	4	6

4

4	7	1	4
5	6	4	1
3	1	6	6
4	2	5	5

A

7	1	4	3
3	8	2	2
1	4	4	6
4	2	5	4

B

3	4	5	2
4	1	6	3
3	7	2	2
4	2	1	7

C

1	2	7	7
8	6	1	2
4	3	5	5
4	6	4	3

D

Place the 26 letters of the alphabet into the grid to make a crossword.

Seven letters have already been placed for you.

A B C D E F G H I J K L M N
O P Q R S T U V W X Y Z

What numbers should replace the letters X and Y?

What numbers should replace the letters X and Y?

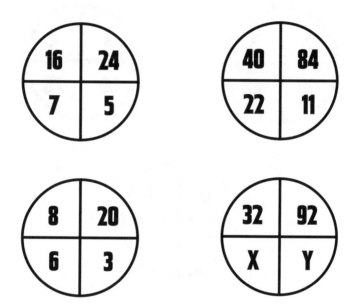

Using the example set in the top grid, what numbers should replace the letters X and Y in the bottom grid?

6	7		3	9	3
	6	6	3		7
6		2	4	6	5
2	4	5	7	1	
5	9	1		8	5
4		5		2	

4	1	4	8		6
	11	2		6	7
3	3	X	7	1	
		3	Y	8	2
2	9	5	1		7
	4		5	4	6

You have left out the plug in the bath, and you are filling the bath with both taps on.

The hot tap takes 6 minutes to fill the bath.
The cold tap takes 4 minutes to fill the bath.
The bath empties in 12 minutes.

In how many minutes will the bath be filled?

Which letter should replace the question mark?

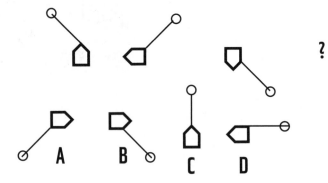

Which of the clocks at the bottom should take the place of the last one in those above?

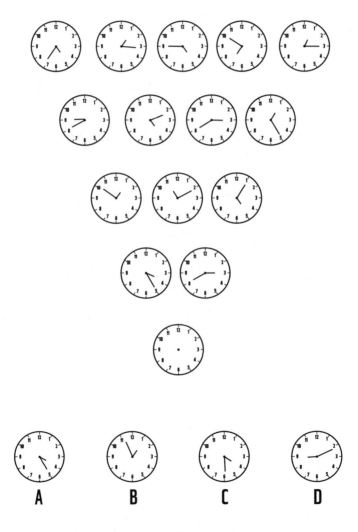

A   B   C   D

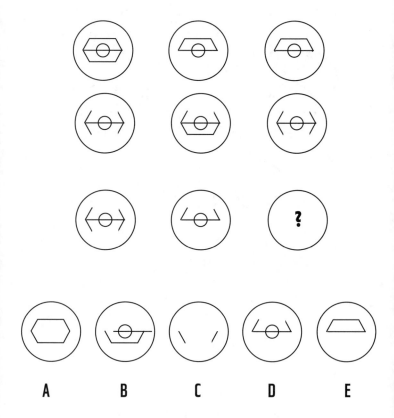

What circle should replace the question mark?

A   B   C   D   E

What number should replace the question mark?

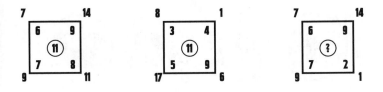

How many 2.5 cm boxes cube can be placed in these three boxes?

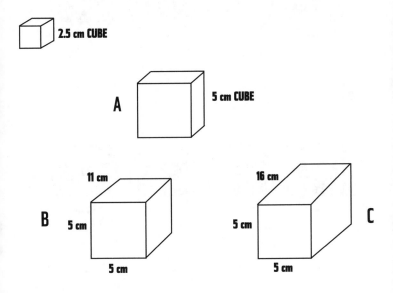

Which of the circles at the bottom should take the place of X?

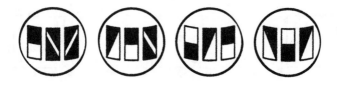

A   B   C   D

Which is the odd one out?

A.	K	N	Q	T	W	Z
B.	B	F	J	N	R	V
C.	A	F	K	P	V	Z
D.	3	6	9	12	15	18
E.	7	11	15	19	23	27
F.	13	18	23	28	33	38

Which bar code is wrong?

A   B   C

D   E   F

What is the total of the square of the lowest number, the square root of the highest number, and the number that is midway between the results?

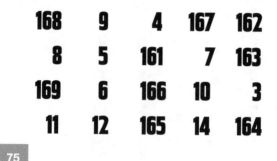

168	9	4	167	162
8	5	161	7	163
169	6	166	10	3
11	12	165	14	164

Which is the odd one out?

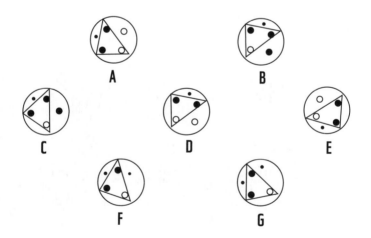

A

B

C

D

E

F

G

Match these into eight pairs.

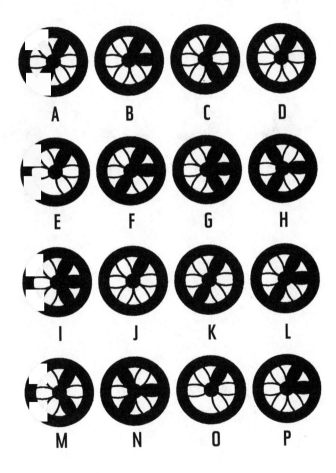

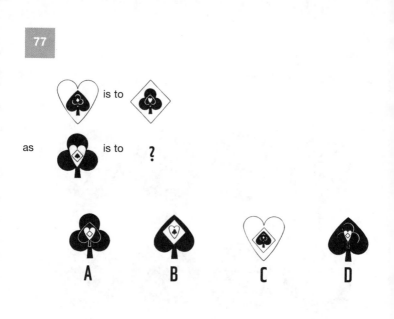

What goes into the empty brackets?

34	(3916)	102
26	(4436)	104
14	( )	70

What number should replace the letter X?

4	7	9	11	8	15	21	6	5
7	6	1	19	11	7	17	8	4
3	11	15	2	9	8	13	10	9
15	8	3	10	4	9	1	3	9
3	13	10	5	1	10	1	6	19
2	12	11	14	5	6	8	3	X

The numbers on the dartboard are arranged as shown below. Add the sum of 10 consecutive numbers that will give the highest total to the sum of 10 consecutive numbers that will give the lowest total.

Workmen, Bob and Frank, were putting the finishing touches to a new door they had fitted to house number 7461. All that was left to do was screw the four metal digits to the door.

"Here's a puzzle for you," said Bob. "Is it possible to screw these four digits on the door in such a way that the four-figure number thus produced cannot be divided by 9 exactly, without leaving a remainder?"

"I don't even have to think about that one," said Frank. "It simply is not possible."

Why did he reply so quickly, and was he correct?

At a local fund raising effort our local Church Club ran a competition where each person who donated received a card with a number of rub-off pictures.

Just one picture has on it the Devil's Head, and only four pictures are identical.

If the four pictures which are identical appear before the Devil's Head appears, then the competitor wins a prize. If, however, the Devil's head is uncovered, then the competitor loses.

There were a total of 35 pictures on the card.

What are the chances of winning?

Which is the odd one out?

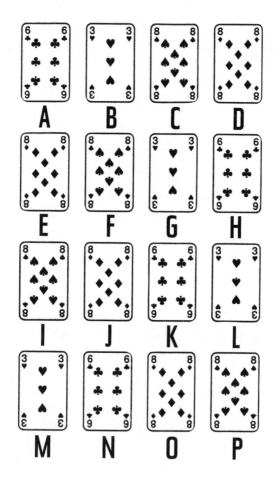

Match these into four pairs:

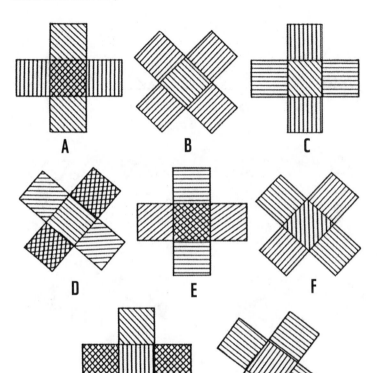

A

B

C

D

E

F

G

H

Which triangle is the odd one out?

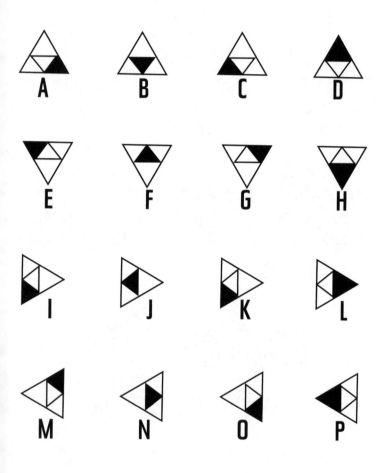

What does this rectangle mean?

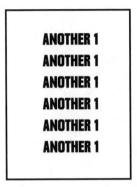

ANOTHER 1
ANOTHER 1
ANOTHER 1
ANOTHER 1
ANOTHER 1
ANOTHER 1

Which of these is the odd one out?

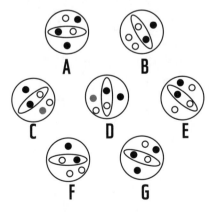

(i) Which globe in the second line should be placed at X?

(ii) Which globe in the bottom line should be placed at Y?

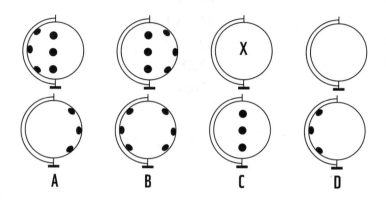

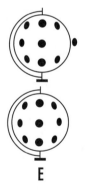  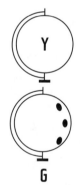 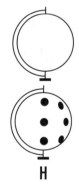

Which figure is wrong?

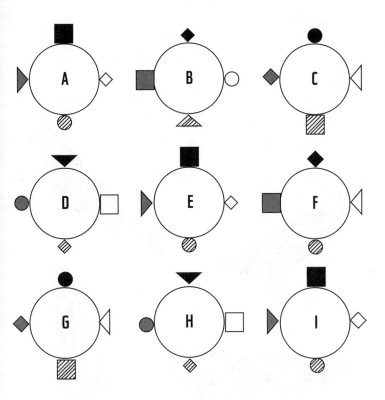

Which shape will complete the hexagon?

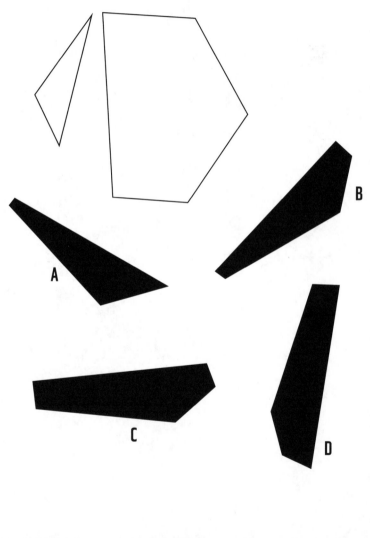

Give values for X, Y and Z.

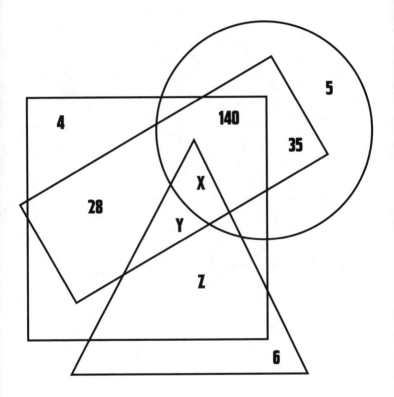

Which is the odd face out?

A

B

C

D

E

F

G

H

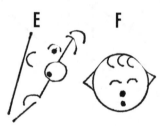

6 3 7 4 is to G F D C, as

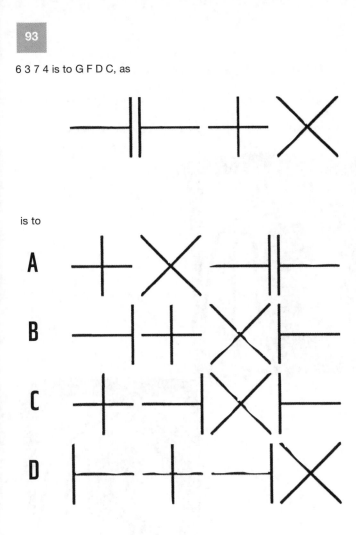

is to

A

B

C

D

Two identical bags each contain eight balls, four white and four black.

One ball is drawn out of bag one and another ball out of bag two.

What are the chances that at least one of the balls will be black?

These columns are indeed crazy, and at first glance there does not appear to be rhyme nor reason in the way the numbers are distributed.

However, on closer inspection can you see a pattern emerging, and can you fill in the bottom row of numbers?

2	2	1	3
4	6	5	5
8	6	9	9
8	12	11	13
14	10	17	15
12	18	17	21
20	14	25	21
16	24	23	29
26	18	33	27
20	30	29	37
32	22	41	33
24	36	35	45
38	26	49	39
?	?	?	?

Which one does not conform?

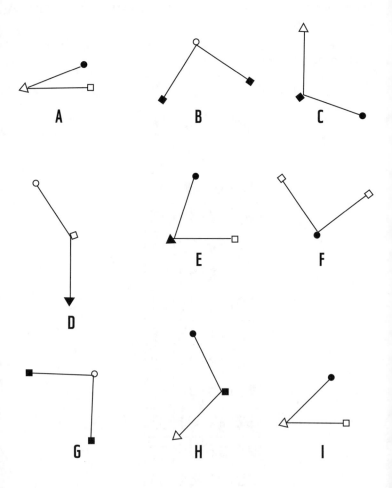

A

B

C

D

E

F

G

H

I

Examine the first four diagrams below and then decide which of the numbered diagrams at the bottom should complete the third row.

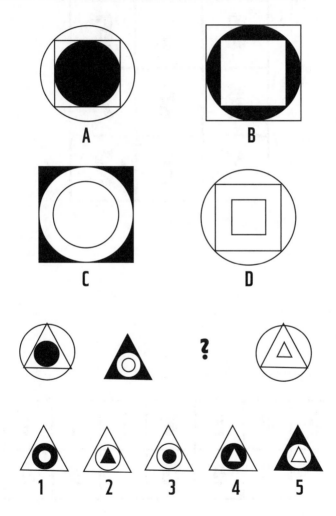

Which numbers should replace the letters X, Y and Z?

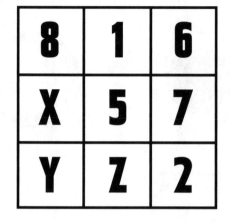

8	1	6
X	5	7
Y	Z	2

What number goes into the empty square?

| 0 | 4 | 5 | 8 | 7 | 1 | 3 |
| | 4 | 9 | 13 | | 8 | 4 |

Which of the numbered symbols at the bottom should take the place of X?

1   6   7

14   7   8

77   98   114

4741   896   X

+ ▽ ∠ □   ◯⊢ ∨
1   2   3   4   5   6   7

Magic Squares can be very intriguing, whether they use number in which each line, column and diagonal adds up to the same number, or whether they use words.

Usually a magic word square consists of a number of different words which can be read both across and down as in the example:

K	I	N	D
I	D	E	A
N	E	A	T
D	A	T	A

However, below is a magic word square with a difference.

Can you fill in the three missing letters so that this is, indeed, a magic word square?

S		I	D
E	I	O	I
R		N	G
P	A		I

This wall has been demolished by a careless driver. Can you reconstruct it from four of the pieces below?

What number logically should replace the question mark?

	15					
				21		24
?			31			
				12	42	
			11			

104

How many different routes are there from A to B?

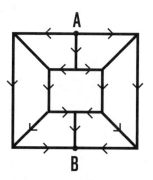

Which vase is wrong?

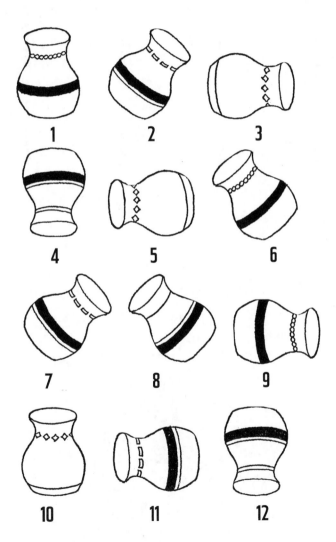

Which one is wrong?

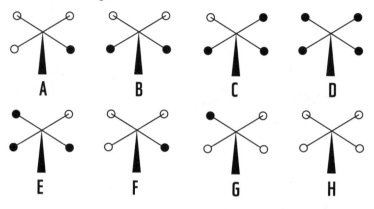

A B C D

E F G H

What should take the place of X?

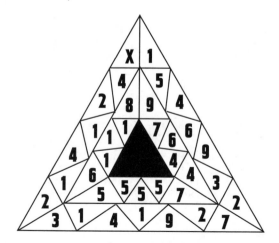

What number should replace the letter X?

Which pattern does not conform with the others?

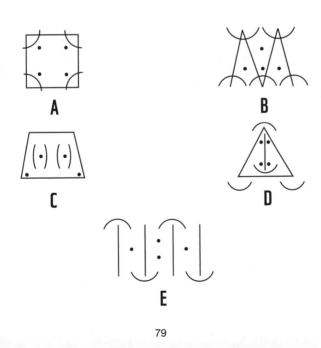

Each of the nine squares in the grid marked 1A to 3C, should incorporate all the lines and symbols which are shown in the squares of the same letter and number immediately above and to the left. For example, 2B should incorporate all the lines and symbols that are in 2 and B.

One of the squares is incorrect. Which is it?

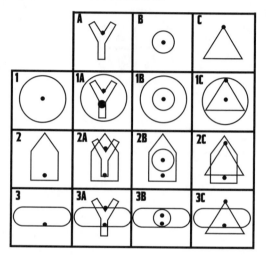

Arrange the four strips into a perfect square, using two each of A, B and C and one of D.

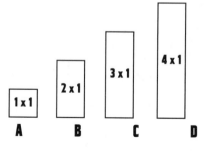

Charlie and Bob were demolishing an old house.

When they reached the children's bedroom they found three stones containing very strange markings.

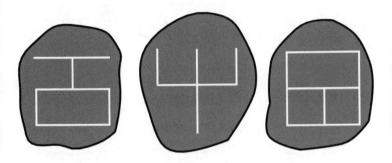

"Must be some sort of hieroglyphics," said Charlie.

"Possibly," said Bob, "but more likely it was one of the children setting a puzzle for one of his brothers or sisters."

"Aha," said Charlie, "and I think I have just solved the puzzle, here's another brick with some more markings, which must be the answer."

What markings did the fourth brick have on it?

Which cup is the odd one out?

A   **B**   **C**

D   **E**   **F**

G   **H**   **I**

Three players each throw three darts that, starting from X, score as follows:

A clockwise: the first three numbers divisible by 3 – all doubles;

B anti-clockwise: the first three numbers divisible by four – all doubles;

C clockwise: the first three numbers divisible by four – all trebles.

What did each player score?

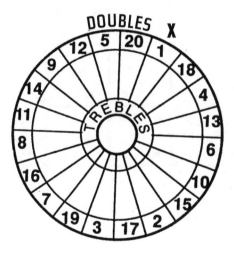

What is the total of the spots on the rear side of these dice?

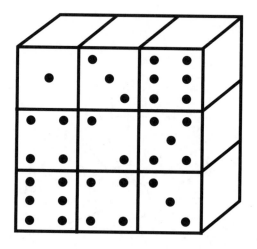

What numbers should take the place f the letters A, B, C and D?

| 3 | 27 | 1 | 32 | 4 | 26 | 3 | 29 |
| 5 | 25 | 5 | 26 | 6 | A | B | C | D |

117

If this shape were folded along the dotted lines it could be made into a cube:

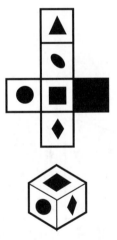

like this:

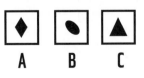

If this cube is turned upside-down, which of these faces will appear at the top?

| ◆ | ⬮ | ▲ |
| A | B | C |

What comes next?

124 **81** **6** **32** **641** **2** **–**

What number should replace the letter X?

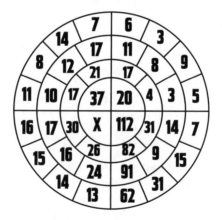

In the game of snakes and ladders the counter is moved according to the throw of the die. When it lands on the foot of a ladder, it moves to the top of the ladder; when it lands on the head of a snake it moves down to the tail. What will be the total of the numbers reached after the following throws of the die? (Do NOT include the squares at the bottom of the ladders or the tops of the snakes in the total, i.e. the first throw = 15, NOT 20):

5   4   4   2   6   3   2   2

100	99	98	97	96	95	94	93	92	91
81	82	83	84	85	86	87	88	89	90
71	72	73	74	75	76	77	78	79	80
61	62	63	64	65	66	67	68	69	70
51	52	53	54	55	56	57	58	59	60
41	42	43	44	45	46	47	48	49	50
31	32	33	34	35	36	37	38	39	40
21	22	23	24	25	26	27	28	29	30
11	12	13	14	15	16	17	18	19	20
1	2	3	4	5	6	7	8	9	10

What number should replace the letter X in the last circle?

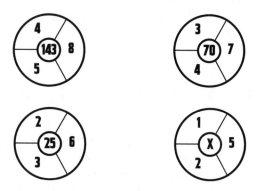

Using only plus or minus signs, arrange the numbers below so that they will equal 10. You must use all the numbers.

3   4   5   6   7   8   9

What will be the result if the hands of this clock are moved as follows:

A. forward 3 hours, 15 minutes

B. back 4 hours, 25 minutes

C. back 1 hour, 30 minutes

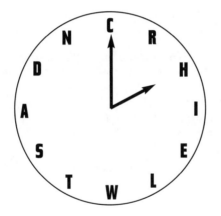

A man is walking his dog on the lead towards home at a steady 4 mph. When they are 10 miles from home the man lets the dog off the lead. The dog immediately runs off towards home at 6 mph. When the dog reaches the house it turns round and runs back to the man at the same speed. When it reaches the man it turns back for the house. This is repeated until the man gets home and lets in the dog. How many miles does the dog cover from being let off the lead to being let in the house?

Here are six clocks turned upside down. Which shows the nearest time to 2.25 if held in front of a mirror? (Don't use a mirror or turn the page.)

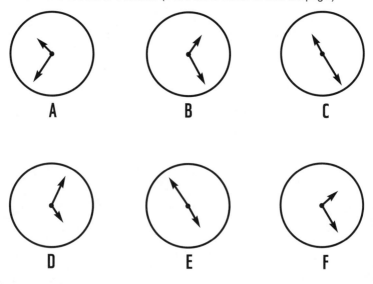

A   B   C

D   E   F

The ball in A moves clockwise, first one letter, then missing one and going onto the next, then missing two, and so on. If it lands on a consonant the ball in B moves to one number clockwise; if it lands on a vowel the ball in B moves to the third number anti-clockwise. If the ball in B lands on an even number the ball in C moves three letters clockwise; if it lands on an odd number the ball in C moves four letters anti-clockwise. What word will be spelt by the ball in C after seven moves?

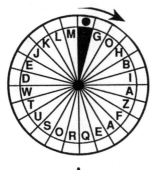

A

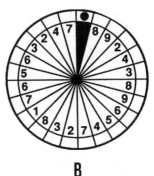

B

C

A boggle puzzle is where a word or a number can be read by moving from square to square horizontally, vertically or diagonally, as distinct from a conventional word search puzzle, where all the words or numbers are read in a straight line. Examples of each are shown below:

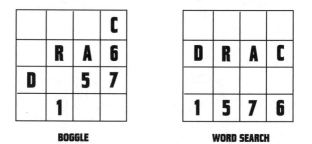

BOGGLE   WORD SEARCH

In the puzzle below consecutive years of the 20th-century are written boggle style, starting with the year 1901 and continuing with subsequent years 1902, 1903, 1904 etc. How many consecutive years of the 20th-century can you find before you get to a missing year? You cannot use a square twice for the same year, however, every square may be used as many times as you wish for different years.

3	8	7	6	4
4	3	2	4	9
9	2	9	0	8
0	1	5	1	7
6	3	9	4	1

My wife usually leaves work at 5.30pm, calls at the supermarket, then catches the 6pm train which arrives at our home town station at 6.30pm. I leave home each day, drive to the station and pick up my wife at 6.30pm just as she gets off the train. One day last week my wife was able to finish work about 10 minutes earlier than usual, decided to go straight to the station instead of calling at the supermarket and managed to catch the 5.30pm train which arrived at our home town station at 6pm. Because I was not there to pick her up she began to walk home. I left home at the usual time, saw my wife walking, turned round, picked her up and drove home, arriving there 12 minutes earlier than usual. For how long had my wife walked before I picked her up?

A colour is concealed in each of these sentences:

A Temper or anger are signs of weakness.

B The money is for Edward.

C You'll find I got it elsewhere.

D One dancer, I see, is out of step.

E 'I'm a gent and a lady's man,' he said.

Give values for X and Y.

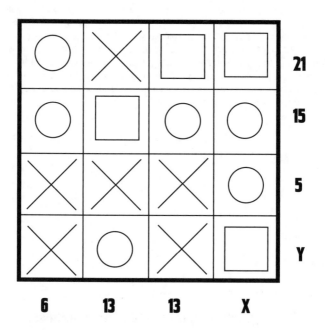

21

15

5

Y

6   13   13   X

Imagine that blocks X and Y are removed from the arrangement below, and that the remaining shape is turned upside-down. Which of the other shapes will be the result?

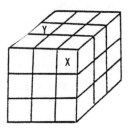

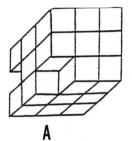

A

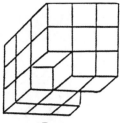

B

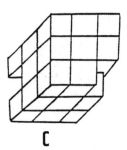

C

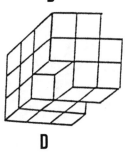

D

Each line and symbol which appears in the four outer circles, in the top diagram, is transferred to the centre circle according to these rules:

If a line or symbol occurs in the outer circles:
once: it is transferred
twice: it is possibly transferred
3 times: it is transferred
4 times: it is not transferred.

Which of the circles A, B, C, D, E, shown below should appear at the centre of the top diagram?

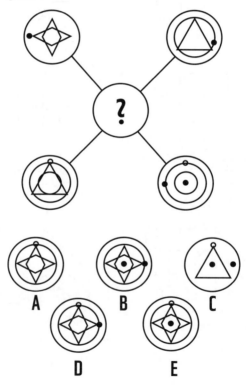

Each of the nine squares in the grid marked 1A to 3C, should incorporate all the lines and symbols which are shown in the squares of the same letter and number immediately above and to the left.

For example, 2B should incorporate all the lines and symbols that are in 2 and B. One of the squares is incorrect. Which one is it?

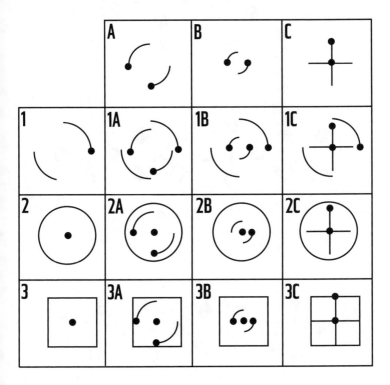

Which is the odd one out?

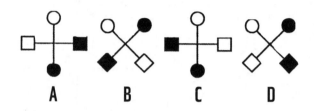

A   **B**   **C**   **D**

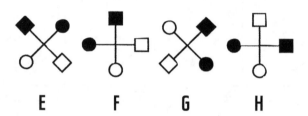

E   **F**   **G**   **H**

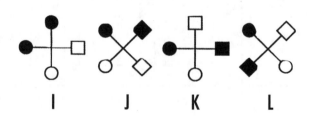

I   **J**   **K**   **L**

Which five of the pieces shown below will form the square?

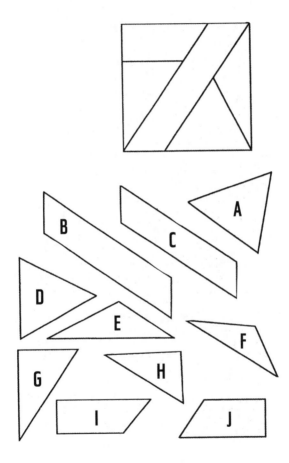

Solutions

1 X is 15; Y is 11

In the outer ring, going clockwise from 7, each number doubles the previous number and subtracts 1. hence x (coming before 29) must be 15. In the inner ring, each number doubles the previous number and adds 1. Hence y is 11 (double 5 plus 1).

2 C

The spiral turns the opposite way from the others.

3 D

All the others contain one acute angle, one obtuse angle and one right angle. D contains two acute angles and on obtuse angle.

4 25

In the first row divide the numbers outside the brackets by 14 and put the results inside the brackets. Continue in the same way, but next dividing by 15 and then by 16. In the last row divide by 17.

5 A is 7, B is 1, C is 8

With a four-figure total, the calculation is obviously addition and not subtraction. In order to reconcile the units with the tens. B must be 1 (the units total 7), so that 7 added to 4 in the tens gives 11, confirming that B is 1 (also confirmed in the final total). To give 2 in the final total, C must be *, so that the hundreds came to 12.

6 4½ or 4.5

In each quarter, halve each total of the rings up to and including the centre. Thus, in the bottom left quarter: 24 plus 12 = 36, 11 plus 7 = 18, 6 plus 3 = 9. Therefore x = 4½ or 4.5.

7 27

In the top line, the first number, 9 is divisible by 3; 8 is divisible by 4; 10 is divisible by 5; 18 is divisible by 6; 21 is divisible by 7; 16 is divisible by 8. hence the next number must be divisible by 9, and the only number that complies with this is 27.

8 99

After the first two terms each subsequent term is the sum of the two previous terms.

9 4

The first term is followed by the last term; the second term is followed by the penultimate term, and the third term follows the same procedure. Thus the series becomes: 25 24 22 19 15 10 4(x) – ie, decreasing by one more each time: -1 -2 -3 -4 -5 -6(x)

10 Matilda   19   Philip   17

11 AD BF CE

12 AIK, BGH, CLN, DEF, JMO

13 $\dfrac{5289 \times (49 + 63) \times 4.5}{60 \times 60}$

$= 739.2 \text{ ft}$

14 2,150
51 is midway between 3 and 99; 43 is midway between 7 and 79; 51 x 43 = 2,193, less 43 (midway between 9 and 77) = 2,150

15 16
Each number in the bottom row is the sum of the number above it and the previous number.

16 Sapphire (2)
    Emerald (5)
    Diamond (10)

17 So that
1. No two consecutive numbers appear in any horizontal, vertical or diagonal line
from which it follows that:
2. No two consecutive numbers appear in adjacent (horizontal, vertical, diagonal) squares.

13	10	7	3
1	4	15	11
8	12	2	6
16	14	5	9

18 38 inches

19 2,519 apples

20 190

21 C
The others are all the same

22 Wind-surfers
(spindrift = spray)

23 A

24 C, D and E

25 F

The design round the top should consist entirely of
diamond shapes, as in B and L. In F one of the diamonds
has become a square.

26 B

The angle is 60º.
The others are 90º, 45º or 30º.

27 3

The numbers following the letters correspond with the position in the alphabet of the letters.

28 16

4 is the square of 2; 9 is the square of 3; 25 is the square of 5; x must be the square of 4 (16).

29 X is 4; Y is 6

Expressing each letter as a number according to its position in the alphabet, the table appears as below, with what were originally letters circled:

(19)	20	+1	
8	(10)		-2
(23)	25	+2	
16	(20)		-4
(1)	4	+3	
5	(11)		-6
(3)	7	+4	
x	12	(x is 4)	-8
(1)	y	+5	(y is 6)
4	(14)		-10

106

30

```
    1 3 0 7 6 0
    1 3 0 7 6 0
    1 3 0 7 6 0
    1 3 0 7 6 0
    1 3 0 7 6 0
+   1 9 4 2 1 5
    8 4 8 0 1 5
```

31 BERLIN

The moves are as follows:

	Ball A	Ball B	Ball C
1st move	19	5	B
2nd move	7	12	E
3rd move	16	6	R
4th move	2	1	L
5th move	20	3	I
6th move	15	16	N

32 245   246   247

Each set of numbers starts by doubling the last number in the previous set and adding first 1, then 2, and so on. The last number in the penultimate set is 120, so the first number in the final set is 245 (240 + 5).

33

Male forenames are:

Leonard

William

David

Jim

Eric

Tom
(Alternate letters in the outer ring)
Female forenames are:
Iris
Mavis
Sarah
Vera
Ann
Amy
(Alternate letters in the inner ring)

34 J
The upper branches should point downwards, as in D, E and N.

35 A
The smallest figure in the centre becomes the largest figure on the outside, while the other figures remain in the same order.

36 2
Spaced correctly the series becomes:
4 9 13 22 35 57 9 (2)
After the first two numbers, each subsequent number is the total of the previous two. The sum of 35 and 57 is 92.

37 B

38 The 9th spin

1st spin	19	
2nd spin	3	
3rd spin		9
4th spin		18
5th spin		32
6th spin		17
7th spin		27
8th spin		3
9th spin		ZERO

39 The figure is turned 45 degrees clockwise each time the black shaded portion moves first from top to bottom (in the first row) and then from left to right (in the second row).

40 E
The wards (the projections at the end) which turn the lock are different from those in the other keys.

41 A 8; B 5; C 7; D 1; E 9; F 3; G 6; H 2; I 4

42 C
The thread turns the opposite way from the others.

43 D
The figure is rotating clockwise.

44 114

The two numbers on the left inside the brackets are the sum of the digits on the left of the brackets. The number on the right inside the brackets is the difference between the sums of the digit on either side of the brackets.

45 AE; BG; CF; DH

46 18

Each modern number in any one segment has a number in Roman numerals in its opposite segment. Starting with MDC (1600), this is doubled in the opposite segment to give 3200. Moving clockwise, IV is halved, to give 2 in the opposite segment. This doubling and halving continues, so by the time we get to IX (9), this must be doubled in the opposite segment to give 18, expressed in modern digits.

47 B

Examination of the top cubes reveals that they are rotating forwards (confirmed by the changed positions of the two spots on the side). As far as the facing side is concerned, B C, D or E could be correct, but only in B have the two spots changed their positions in keeping with the forward rotation.

48 71

Each number is increased by adding the total of its digits to the number itself. So, 11 (1 + 1 = 2) becomes 13, 13 (1 + 3 = 4) becomes 17, etc.

Following this procedure, 58 (5 + 8 = 13) becomes 71.

49 2

50 38 (5 x 4) + (10 + 8)

51 SPINNAKER

52 6,561
There are two sequences arranged alternately. In each
sequence the number is the square of the previous number
in that sequence. 6,561 is the square of 81.

53 A ½ revolution
B 2½ revolutions.

54 B

55 D

56 E
B is the same as D; A is thesame as C

57 Colony of Frogs
    Horde of Gnats
    Den of Snakes
    Clutter of Spiders

Nest of Machine Guns
Park of Artillery
Doylt of Swine
Gang of Elks
Business of Ferrets
Volery of Birds
Hover of Crows
Drift of Wild Pigs

58 40mph

59 12
Opposite faces of the dice add up to 7. Therefore, moving horizontally from left to right and starting in the top row, opposite faces are: 3 1 6 2.

60 B
All the rows, horizontally and vertically add as follows:

Square 1   19
Square 2   18
Square 3   17
Square 4   16

In square B all the rows, horizontally and vertically, add to 15.
Alternatively, the numbers in square 1 add to 76. Those in square 2 add to 72. Those in sqyuare 3 add to 68, and in square 4 they add to 64. Therefore (decreasing by 4 each time) square H (60) must follow square 4.

62 X is 11; Y is 61

In the first circle the number in the top left quarter is squared and then reduced by 1 in the opposite diagonal quarter; the number in the top right quarter is cubed and then 1 added to give the number in the opposite lower quarter.

In the second circle the same procedure is followed except that 2 is deducted from the squared number and 2 is added to the cubed number.

Therefore, in the third circle 3 is deducted from the square of 8 (64 becomes 61 – the value for Y), while 3 is added to the cube of 2 (8 becomes 11 – the value for X).

63 X is 9 or 24; Y also is 9 or 24

In each case the numbers at the top are divided by 4 in the opposite quarter and 1 is added.

An alternative solution is that the numbers in the lower quarters are miltiplied by 4 in their opposite quarters and 4 is deducted from the result.

64 X = 5; Y = 4

From the top square:

2 numbers total 13

3 numbers total 15

4 numbers total 17

5 numbers total 19

In the bottom square:

X is in a row of five and must be 5 to bring the total (14) up to 19;

Y is in a row of four and must be 4 to bring the total (13) up to 17.

65 3 minutes

Take reciprocals

$6 = \frac{1}{6}$ = .166

$4 = \frac{1}{4}$ = <u>.25</u>

+   .416

$12 = \frac{1}{12}$ = <u>.083</u>

-         .333

$\frac{1}{333}$ = 3 -

66 A 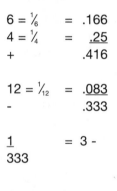 moves 90° clockwise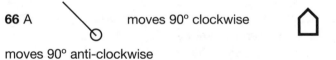

moves 90° anti-clockwise

67 C

In the top row the total of the hours to which the hands point is 50 (12, 4, 13, 17 and 4); in the second row the total is 40 (17, 6, 11 and 6); in the third row the total is 30 (11, 13 and 6); in the fourth row the total is 20 (9 and 11). Hence, in the bottom clock the total must be 10, and C (4 and 6) is the only one that gives this.

68 D

69 7

(7 + 14 + 9 + 1) - (6 + 9 + 7 +2)

70 A 8

B 16

C 24

71 C

The first five patterns indicate that they are globes, rotating anti-clockwise.

72 C

In A two letters are missed out.

In B three letters are missed out.

In C four letters are missed out with the exception of V, which should be U.

The numbers in D, E and F follow the same pattern.

73 B

74 33

75 E

76 A-K, B-P, C-M, D-J, E-O, F-L, G-I and H-N.

77 B
The very small centre suit becomes the large outer suit. The next smallest inner suit becomes the next largest outer suit. The next smallest inner suit becomes the next largest outer suit. The largest outer suit becomes the smallest centre suit.

78 5116
Divide the number on the right outside the brackets by the number on the left outside the brackets to give the first number inside the brackets. The two digits on the right inside the brackets are the square of the right-hand digit of the number on the left outside the brackets. The remaining digit (the second inside the brackets) is the square of the digit on the left of the number on the left outside the brackets.

79 9

80 210

81 The reason Frank replied so quickly is that he had spotted that the digits 7 - 4 - 6 - 1 add up to 18, and when the sum of the digits is divisible by 9 exactly, then the number itself is also divisible by 9 exactly. Therefore, in whatever order you arrange these four digits, the number produced will divide exactly by 9.

82 4/1 against.
The number of pictures on the card does not affect the odds. The only thing that does affect the odds are the number of winning pictures and the number of losing pictures.

83 L
The middle heart has been changed to a spade.

84 AE, BH, CF, DG

85 K
Each row follows the same pattern of shading as in the first row, except for K, which should appear as in C, G and O.

86 One after another.

87 E

A is the same as G, B is the same as F; C is the same as D.

88 (i) Globe A; (ii) Globe G

The globes are rotating anti-clockwise.

In (i) there are two vertical rows of spots situated adjacent to each other. At X one of these rows (the centre one on the first globe) will be on the blind side and only one row will be visible.

In (ii) there are three vertical rows of spots on one side of the globe only. On the other side there are no spots. Therefore at Y there will be one row visible, while in the next position of the globe all three rows will be on the blind side.

89 The figure rotates $\frac{1}{4}$ turn anti-clockwise. the difference in shading remains constant throughout. In F the small outer circle and the triangle have changed places.

90 B

91 X = 840

Y = 168

Z = 24

Values of the shapes as indicated are: square = 4, circle = 5, and triangle = 6. The value of the rectangle is not indicated, but is obviously 7. This is ascertained from the relationship between 4 (square) and 28, or 5 (circle) and 35. From this it can also be seen that the values of overlapping areas are obtained by multiplying the values of the individual shapes that make up those areas.

Confirmation of this is given by 140, which is the product of 4, 5 and 7.

Therefore, X is the product of the circle, square, triangle and rectangle; Y is the product of the triangle, rectangle and square; Z is the product of the triangle and square.

92 H

The faces are made up of four straight lines, five curves, two dots and one circle. In H there are only three straight lines.

93 C

Substitute numbers for letters according to their alphabetic position. Thus, the first relationship is between 6 3 7 4 and 7 6 4 3. The figures at the bottom are transposed in the same order.

94 Three chances in four.
The possible combinations are:

> black - black
> white - white
> black - white
> white - black

There is only one of these combinations where black does not occur, therefore the chances of drawing at least one black ball are three chances in four.

95 28, 42, 41, 53
Four sequences alternate between columns:
Columns A & C
2, 5, 8, 11, 14 etc
Columns B & A
2, 4, 6, 8, 10 etc
Columns C & D
1, 5, 9, 13 ,17 etc
Columns D & B
3, 6, 9, 12, 15 etc

96 E
Acute angles have symbols at the end of the lines, as
shown in the first row. Obtuse angles and right angles have
different symbols.
In the second row the colours of the symbols are reversed
(black becoming white and white becoming black), and in
the third row they are reversed again.
Therefore, in E the circle and square are the wrong colours.

97 A, B, C and D are made up of circles and squares.
In A there is a circle inside a square inside a circle;
In B there is a square inside a circle inside a square;
In C there is a circle inside a circle inside a square;
In D there is a square inside a square inside a circle.
The third row is made up of triangles and circles,
conforming in the same way.
In A the centre figure (the circle) is black; in B the middle
figure (the circle) is black; in C the outer figure (the square)
is black; in D none of the figures is black.
The third row must conform in the same way.

98 X= 3

Y = 4

Z = 9

The total of each line, horizontally, vertically and diagonally will then be 15.

99 15

The lower number is the sum of the number above it and its preceding number.

100 Number 2.

In the first row there is one horizontal line (in the 7),
one vertical line (in the 1), one diagonal line (in the 7) and one circle (in the 6).

In the second line there are two of each.

In the third line there are three of each.

In the fourth line there are four of each.

There ARE four circles (in 896), but only three vertical horizontal and diagonal lines. Number 2 is the only figure which supplies all three.

101 Put the letter T in each blank space. Now start at the bottom left hand square and read up the first column, then along the top and eventually spiralling into the centre to spell out the word prestidigitation. A very magic word presented very squarely indeed!

102 A, B J and K

103 42

Each number represents its position in the square relative to the other numbers. So 21 has two blank squares above it and one blank square below it.

104 10

105 8

A vase with a broad black band round the centre has a row of circles round its neck; if there is a broad black band with a thin line below it round the centre, there is a row of rectangles round the neck; if there is a thin line near the bottom of the vase there is a row of diamonds near the neck.

When there is a broad black band round the centre with a thin line above it there should be a double line going round the neck, but in number 8 there is only a single line.

106 F

In the first row the balls are arranged as follows:

A: 1 black ball; B: 2 black balls; C: 3 black balls; D: 4 black balls.

In the second row the WHITE balls should follow the same arrangement, so that F should have two white balls instead of three.

107 3

The total of the numbers on each side of the large triangle should be the same as the total on the same side of the small triangle. The total of the numbers on the left-hand side of the small triangle is 17, made up of 8, 1, 1, 1 and 6. The numbers given on the side of the large triangle are 2, 1, 4, 1, 2 and 4, giving a total of 14. Therefore the remaining number must be 3, to bring the total up to 17.

108 X= 420
Opposite numbers are obtained by multiplying the smaller number by one less than itself. In the first circle: 3 multiplied by 2 gives 6 and 8 multiplied by 7 gives 56; in the second circle 9 multiplied by 8 gives 72 and 12 multiplied by 11 gives 132. In the third circle 14 multiplied by 13 gives 182 and 21 multiplied by 20 gives 420.

109 B
Each pattern consists of four straight lines, four curves and four dots, except B, which has five curves.

110 1A. There is a dot missing.

111

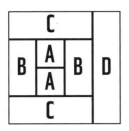

112

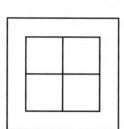

They are the numbers 2, 4, 6, 8 with mirror-image.

113 G
The handle is in the wrong position, as compared with B and D.

114 A scores 78
B scores 80
C scores 84

115 29
Opposite faces of a die add up to 7. Therefore, moving horizontally from left to right and starting in the top row, opposite faces are: 6 4 1 3 5 2 1 3 4

116 A is 24; B is 7; C is 23; D is 7
There are four series. Starting with the first term and taking every fourth term thereafter:
3 4 5 6 7(d)
Starting with the second term and continuing in the same way:

27 26 25 24(a)
Starting with the third term:
1 3 5 7(b)
Starting with the fourth term:
32 29 26 23 (c)

117 C

118 8
This is an ordinary 'doubling-up' series, but wrongly
spaced. When correctly spaced, the answer becomes
obvious: 1 2 4 8 16 32 64 128

119 55
In each quarter, add the numbers in the outer ring, then
those in the next ring, and then the next.
In the top left quarter these totals descend:
40 39 38 37 (the single number in the centre).
In the top right quarter they descend:
23 22 21 20 (the single number in the centre)
In the right lower quarter they descend:
115 114 113 112 (the single number in the centre).
Therefore, in the lower left quarter they descend:
58 57 56 – and then, 55 (X).

120 271

1st throw (5) becomes	15
2nd throw (4) becomes	19
3rd throw (4) becomes	4

4th throw (2) becomes	28
5th throw (6) becomes	72
6th throw (3) becomes	93
7th throw (2) becomes	38
8th throw (2) becomes	2
	271

121 X is 2
The number in the inner circle is the difference between the product and the sum of the three numbers in the outer circle.

122 Because only plus and minus signs are used there are many possible arrangements of these numbers.
Four examples are:
3+8-7+6-5+9-4
8-6-7+5+9+4-3
4-3+9+8+5-7-6
9-5+6-7+8+3-4

Any permutation of the numbers shown above (with the appropriate signs) would have satisfied the question. Of course, if division or multiplication had been required, the number of possible answers would have been very limited.

123 CHILDREN
Present time indicated – CH, A. Forward to 5.15 – IL, B. Back to 12.50 – DR, C. Back to 11.20 – EN.

124 15 miles
The man walks 10 miles at 4 mph = 2.5 hours
The dog runs 2.5 hours at 6mph and covers 15 miles

125 D

126 JONQUIL
The moves result as follows:

	Ball A	Ball B	Ball C
1st move	G	8	J
2nd move	H	9	O
3rd move	A	4	N
4th move	E	6	Q
5th move	U	7	U
6th move	K	6	I
7th move	I	8	L

127 1901-1954. It is not possible to read 1955 boggle style.

128 24 minutes
As I leave according to my usual schedule, it must be before 6.30pm when I pick up my wife. Because we have saved 12 minutes, that must be the time that it takes me to drive from the point I picked her up to the station, and back to that same point. Assuming it takes me an equal 6 minutes each way, I have, therefore, picked her up 6 minutes before I would normally do so, which means 6.24pm. So my wife must have walked from 6pm to 6.24 pm or for 24 minutes.

129 A Orange
B Red
C Indigo
D Cerise
E Magenta

130 X is 22 and Y is 13
Fairly simple deduction, especially if you realized that there
were no alternatives in the third horizontal row, which led to
the solution for the first vertical row.

131 B
Removing blocks X and Y leaves the following: diagram
Turned upside-down, this corresponds with B.

132 B. The diamond occurs once vertically and once
horizontally. The dot occurs on the right and in the centre.

133 2B (dot missing)

134 I

135 A, B, E, G and J